The Savvy Presenter

100 Tips for Mastering Presentations

Joanne G. Linowes

images
Publishing

Dedication
To David F. and Dorothy W. for the foundation
To L. David for the inspiration
To Shelby, Robert, Jason for the perpetuation

Published in Australia in 2010 by
The Images Publishing Group Pty Ltd
ABN 89 059 734 431
6 Bastow Place, Mulgrave, Victoria 3170, Australia
Tel: +61 3 9561 5544 Fax: +61 3 9561 4860
books@imagespublishing.com
www.imagespublishing.com

Copyright © The Images Publishing Group Pty Ltd 2010
The Images Publishing Group Reference Number: 872

National Library of Australia Cataloguing-in-Publication entry:

Author:	Linowes, Joanne.
Title:	The savvy presenter: 100 tips for mastering presentations Joanne Linowes; illustrator Bob Gill.
ISBN:	9781864703610
Notes:	Includes index.
Subjects:	Business presentations.
Other Authors/Contributors:	Gill, Bob.
Dewey Number:	658.452

Coordinating editor: Robyn Beaver

Designed by The Graphic Image Studio Pty Ltd, Mulgrave, Australia
www.tgis.com.au

Digital production and print by Everbest Printing Co Ltd. in Hong Kong/China
Printed on 157gsm GoldEast Matt Art paper

IMAGES has included on its website a page for special notices in relation to this and our other publications. Please visit www.imagespublishing.com.

Contents

Introduction

The ability to present ideas effectively and compellingly is a valued skill. This handy book of quick tips goes beyond basic presentation skills to provide the potency and fine-tuning required for turning a good presentation into an influential, impressive presentation.

These 100 tips are not your standard presentation hints—they are the pointers to put your presentations over the top.

For a presentation to flow and appeal, to spark thinking and engage, to be well-targeted and hit the mark, the presenter weaves together a variety of techniques for the specific occasion and audience. Like a jigsaw puzzle, fitting the right pieces results in the perfect combination to affect each listener—to move decision-makers to action, or to inform, to build understanding, to accomplish the task, to meet the goal.

Different combinations of tips will work best at different times. Every presentation is an opportunity to select and blend hints from this book that help you make the impression that counts.

These 100 tips are just a part of the author's comprehensive family of presentation methodologies. Developed continuously since 1986, these copyrighted techniques have proven successful with thousands of professionals and business people in Fortune 500 companies, ENR 500 design firms, nonprofit associations, small professional firms, and in university courses.

The power of these 100 tips is maximized when used in conjunction with the author's presentation coaching and professional development programs. This book serves both as a personal ready-reference and as a resource in the author's continuing education seminars.

Great presenters are made, not born. Whether your presentations are competitive, convincing, or informational; are for clients, prospects, decision-makers, law-makers, the community, or for colleagues at professional meetings; are in formal settings or in informal meetings and team task groups; whatever your presentation, when you are clear, concise, and compelling you can watch your listeners come alive, your plans be accepted, and your career zoom ahead. Put these 100 tips to work for you!

Please visit **www.savvypresenter.com** to find more presentation tips to help you succeed and to help your company prosper.

Set your compass

The ultimate goal of the savvy presenter is to guide people to take some sort of action, do broader thinking, or come to a new conclusion. Your presentation must help listeners decide what's important, what makes sense, what they want, or how they should proceed. Ask yourself, "What do I want them to do as a result of hearing me?"

Keep this goal as your compass as you prepare and deliver information.

TIP #2

Make it snappy!

A powerful presentation involves more than just the effective delivery of important content. Blend substance with public relations **pizzazz** and the *human touch*. Think beyond content to create lively, stimulating approaches to pique interest. Consider each decision-maker as an individual whom you want to reach, teach, and engage.

Double or nothing

Compose your presentation with two guideposts: make your point *and* create chemistry. *Apply structure **and** project stature.*

Structure requires following a specific, orderly approach to organizing your information.

Stature requires radiating personality while maintaining poise and expertise. Unless you intertwine structure and stature, your presentation will fall flat.

Get started

For a high-stakes presentation, start your preparation with three elements before developing the content:

- Learn the motives and underlying viewpoints of your audience.

- Plan presentation components with your end goal firmly in mind.

- Brainstorm various methods to make the presentation distinctive.

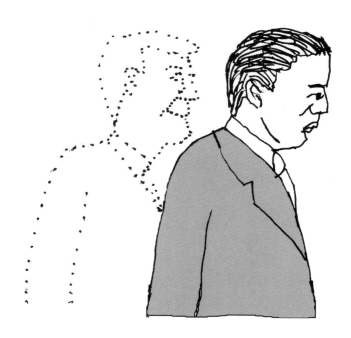

Switch viewpoint

Mentally step around to the listeners' side and hear your subject matter from their viewpoint. Put yourself in the audience. Are you relating to *their* interests and needs? Are you addressing *their* concerns? Do you connect with their personal risks and rewards pertaining to this topic?

View from the top

To influence decision-makers, start preparation by thinking beyond *your* goal of getting the decision or nudging an action. Envision the 30,000-foot view from the listener's perspective. Ask yourself, "How does this subject matter fit in the individual's big picture?" Consider the ramifications of the information for decision making in the broader profession, the entire community, or the whole organization.

TIP #7

Think construction

Construct your presentation using a linear, bullet-point structure that makes your information clear and easily grasped.

A story is not a structure

Contrary to popular belief, an influential presentation is not structured by telling a story. A story is *one device* you can use as part of your explanation, a way to drive the point home or make it stick. Story-telling format is not an effective arrangement of ideas for the presentation as a whole.

TIP #9

What's the problem?

Phrase your opening statement as a problem you are asked to solve.

Begin with vigor

Open with a confident, energized voice. In the first 12 seconds, *the* impression is created.

You can influence reaction to your entire presentation with your opening voice.

TIP #11

How or why?

Position yourself as the valuable resource. State the situation as a problem-to-be-solved in a single question beginning with "how" or "why." Then proceed throughout the presentation to answer the question.

Reach the real decision-maker

Is the *real* decision-maker in the room during your presentation? If not, that affects how you prepare and deliver. Encourage those who hear you first-hand to become your emissaries. They must be able to transfer your message and your passion to another person in another context.

Arm your emissaries

When the real decision-maker is not in the room, craft ways to help those who must carry the message onward and deliver it on point to the one individual who has the power.

Create:

- Short, easy-to-remember main points.

- A memorable theme.

- An air of enthusiasm.

- A targeted statement of benefits to the end-user.

In the end, it's special delivery

Let your last line be important and enthusiastic. Deliver your concluding sentence with a strong voice, sincere eyes, and open body language. Your final statement is an energized reminder of the essence of your message and the effectiveness of *you*.

Be compelling

Be able to state your issue, proposal, action, or idea in a succinct sentence of 15–18 words, max. Place this statement in a strategic location in your presentation. Use a dynamic voice to make it stand out.

TIP #16

Anticipate potential boomerangs

Plan your content with an eye toward the unexpected, defensive, heated, or nonproductive response. Work to address these negatives in the body of your presentation while you have control. If these issues slip into the question-and-answer session, it is harder to turn the negatives into the positives you need.

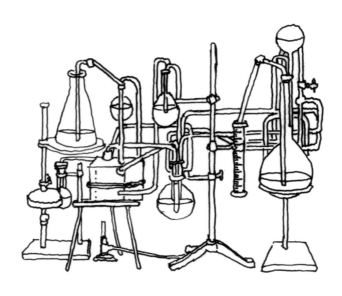

Create chemistry

The more listeners respect and admire the speaker, the greater confidence they are likely to place in anything the speaker says, and therefore, the more prone they are to adopt the suggestions.

TIP #18

Drop in a credential nugget

Regardless of your position or job title, you cannot assume that everyone in the room knows the depth of your expertise on the topic. When preparing, select a very few of your most relevant credentials and excellent examples of your expertise. Plan how you will casually drop them into your remarks at appropriate places. Just a few nuggets are plenty—be careful not to overdo it.

Stand or sit?

If in doubt, stand when you present. When appropriate, if you choose to start while seated, create opportunities to stand by demonstrating something or pointing on a visual.

Try to conclude while standing—you can then, if desired, nonchalantly slide into your seat for the question-and-answer portion.

Choreography counts

Choreograph the whole experience, from
your initial entrance to the final exit. Resolve
beforehand how you will manipulate your time,
your speaking space, your handout materials,
your visuals, your informal chatting, your*self*.

Art Center College Library
1700 Lida Street
Pasadena, CA 91103

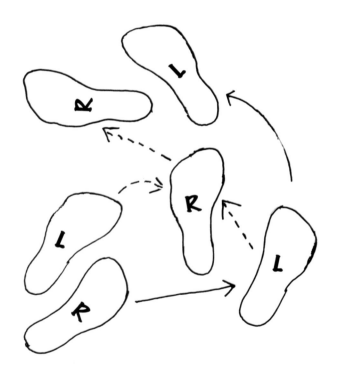

Don't just stand there

Before you start speaking, take a look at your speaking space and determine two or three well-positioned places to stand. While speaking, move comfortably between them so you vary your location and stance. You will want to include one spot near your visuals so you can point or change slides and one spot as close to the audience as you dare.

Interact with the visuals

Beyond pointing, interact with your graphics, presentation boards, whiteboard, easel flipchart. If possible, actually draw on the image to emphasize a point or note a location. On maps, aerial photos, or timelines, draw to indicate movement, distance, size, or timespan.

Don't prepare in a vacuum

With a power presentation, find out more about your audience than you would for a general presentation. Dig to uncover what will turn them on, what will turn them off, and how this project fits into their big picture.

Give 'em the strong arm

Put **strength** in your gestures! Tense your biceps and hand muscles when you point to your visuals. Tighten your shoulder muscles when you move around as well as when you stand still. Keep your voice conversational while your body says "I mean business."

Learn their language

Learn how the decision-makers in your audience describe things: do they refer to "issues," "problems," "challenges," or "obstacles"? Listen to how they speak and then use their terminology when presenting to them. This breaks through one of the major communication barriers.

Direct them to the treasure

Always include a statement about benefits of your ideas/plan to the end user. Listeners may not automatically figure this out from your presentation. Describe the benefits directly.

Be conversational

Think conversation, not memorization. Rehearse to learn the ideas, the order, and the flow. The wording does not need to be exactly the same every time you review your remarks. Of course, when you have specifically honed phrases, politically correct wording, and precise facts that need to be memorized, they still must be delivered conversationally. It takes practice.

Offer a sneak preview

At the outset, the savvy presenter will provide a preview of the main points. It is best not only to state them aloud, but also to display the points in visual format. That way, all can see how the presentation will proceed and observe these as the key points to remember.

This is different from an agenda. This displays the main content points you want listeners to retain.

Provide hand-outs and leave-behinds

Always provide some type of hand-out material for general listeners as well as decision-makers to take away from the presentation. Simple, easy-to-follow hand-outs become simple, easy-to-refer-to reference materials when back at the desk. Provide agenda-style hand-outs at the outset of the presentation. At the end, provide materials that require concentration.

Distribute a useful item that will not immediately become trash.

Play *the* power card

Tell people not what you want to tell them, but what they *need to know* in order to make the decision, be better informed, take the next step, or follow-up.

Put the status report in a compartment

When you need to bring the audience up to speed before you actually begin the heart of your subject matter, create a separate compartment or segment of your presentation in which to give the status report or project update. Be succinct. Include a list of accomplishments or milestones.

Connect from your closet

Soften rough rapport and create a perception of approachability with clothing in earth tones that downplay contrast and are similar in hue.

TIP #33

Do it now!

Build in a sense of "urgency" and importance.

TIP #34

Surprise!

Include the unexpected, a surprise element.
This might be an unanticipated benefit or
broader application of your idea or plan.
Or, it might be an unusual delivery technique
or exciting, different activity that you just pop
in while you are presenting.

Power garb

Grab power garb from your closet. Put the psychology of attire on your side. When you need to appear the most authoritative and credible, wear high-contrast colors—black and white are the ultimate!

Tone your voice

Use tone of voice to affect how you want your audience to react. Different emotions result from different vocal tones—try a serious sound, friendly quality, upbeat enthusiastic tone, in-charge intonation, and so on. Decide the frame of mind best suited to your presentation goal and speak in the tone that elicits your desired response.

Use vivid language

The dynamic power of a suggestion will be greater the more concretely and vividly the suggestion is made.

TIP #38

Make the suggestion, again

Strengthen your suggestion. The appeal of a suggestion varies with the frequency with which it is met. Use repetition. How? Keep the message consistent while giving it a fresh face. Vary the format, medium, style, and wording.

TIP #39

Let them decide

Format your subject matter so it helps listeners process information effectively.

Use *either/or* to evaluate options.

Use *pros/cons* to balance differences or conflict.

Use *card-stacking* to offer all the reasons in favor of a decision and few against it.

Have an attitude

Embrace a new attitude to expand your presentation role so you become:

You—the ambassador for your endeavor.

You—the problem solver.

You—the reputation-builder for your organization.

TIP #41

Point with your voice

Make ears perk up at the critical points. Get the
key information noticed! Punch specific words,
draw out selected phrases, pause before or after
key ideas are expressed.

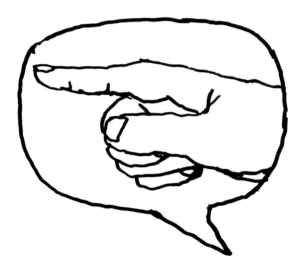

TIP #42

Plan for spontaneity

Include phrasing, in even the most formal presentation, that makes the idea sound lively and spontaneous. The appeal of your plan or recommendations depends on how conversational and personable it seems when you present it. Plan your "spontaneous" talking points ahead.

Engage

Dominate with your eyes, hands, and voice.

TIP #44

Be sure-footed

Deliver with your personality. Act confident even if you don't feel it. If you act confident, the listener will believe you are and will be more inclined to consider your ideas.

TIP #45

Mix media

Listeners respond well to variety of media.
So, no need to rely on just one media format
per presentation. Mix in various media to
keep the presentation lively while reinforcing
your points.

Try combinations of two or three from a long list of options, such as: presentation boards, video clips, still photos, graphics, computer animation, two presenters in dialogue, props, readings, table-top graphics, models, audio segments, white board, easel flipchart hand-drawings, attractive renderings, role plays, aerial images, sound effects, facilitated discussion, interactive exercises, small group problem solving, debate, workshop activities ...

TIP #46

Save the best for last

The most common approach in building a presentation is to decide on the visuals first and then wrap the presentation around them. Wrong. Begin by determining which main points to cover and flesh out the content. THEN, as the *last* step, decide which visuals help make your point and make the case convincingly.

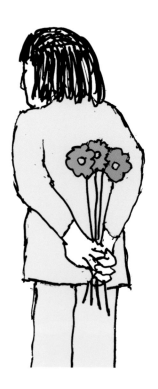

Enlist power words

Replace drab words with ear-catching language. An elaborate vocabulary is not required. Make time to find the word or phrase that transforms a regular sentence into a more effective expression.

Drab:

Our work will meet your highest standards.

The components of this plan are …

Grab:

We deliver with precision you can count on.

The *features* of this plan are …

Make solid statements

Add numbers, percentages, and statistics strategically (and sparingly). These powerful tools solidify broad or vague statements and authenticate claims.

Drab:

Recently, a number of our staff have completed many similar projects.

Grab:

Within the last 18 months, our staff completed four $2.9m projects, each with specifications similar to yours.

Unclog your message

Overloading with numbers, percentages, statistics, graphs, and charts will clog your message and drown your main points. More numbers do not necessarily result in greater validation. Plan how each number you include will make the point. Be strict in deciding how much you need to impress your listeners.

Streamline the dense

Visuals thick with text and quantitative information need verbal explanation. For each densely filled visual, select 1–3 specific items; call attention by highlighting them on the visual and stating in one sentence why each selected item is important.

Eliminate the stuffing

Avoid the temptation to stuff your presentation with visuals/slides for every point. The visuals that add the most value are those that provide structure for your talk, reinforce key points, clarify complex information, and create the atmosphere.

Add life!

Add the *people* component to certain presentations. Step away from the projected image and use hand motions blended with voice to illustrate your point. Or, you can find ways to involve others, such as having two presenters dialogue, including a show-of-hands audience survey, or introducing an impromptu question-and-answer session (town hall style) with previously selected participants in the midst of your formal presentation.

Blank is beautiful

Create tremendous impact in your projected presentation by using blank slides. Let your personality and presence make the statement without distraction.

- Insert blank slides when you need to make a strong appeal.

- Insert blank slides when you need to ask for support or ask listeners to take action.

TIP #54

Avoid same old same old

In discussing your plans or ideas, emphasize what is new! Innovative! More comprehensive! More cutting-edge! Discuss why your proposal or suggestion is a step ahead of former approaches and competing ideas.

Make your statement. Then sit down

There is no presentation that is too short. Just think of the impact of President Lincoln's Gettysburg Address. Be brief. To the point. Memorable.

TIP #56

Watch the clock

Running out of time? Don't say, "In the interest of time we'll stop here." Or, "In the interest of time, I won't discuss …" If you are talking too long, don't admit that to the audience. Just move smoothly and quickly to your planned ending.

TIP #57

Start and end with no back-up

Deliver your opening few sentences and concluding statement against a blank screen. The beginning paragraph and your last sentence are pivotal points for cementing that valuable, personalized connection.

Let your body talk

With a friendly, yet definitive demeanor, let your body make the statement, "Listen up, I have something important to say."

Hold up your head, pull up your chin(s), straighten your back, smile.

Think "show business"

Act like you love presenting!

TIP #60

No crowding

When creating visuals, less is more. Keep open space around words. Keep graphs and charts simple and easy to read. Use no more than three photos or images per board or slide, each one large enough to prominently demonstrate your point. Visuals help clarify information, so keep them clutter-free.

Use projected slides like a pro

Guidelines for slide design:

- Slash the number of words on each slide to the barest minimum. If people are busy reading your slide they cannot listen at 100 percent.

- Be disciplined. Delete extraneous logos/images/graphics.

- Select high-contrast combinations for background and text colors—let the lettering stand out.

Max person-to-person power

Make projected visuals and graphics work for *you*:

- Avoid being simply the narrator for your slide show.

- Add the human touch: talk *with* and look *at* your audience.

- Give people ample time to read the slide or examine the graphic.

- Punctuate with your voice.

Prop it up

Use props as evidence and to demonstrate.
Bring in examples of reports, publications,
models, samples—anything that makes your
words tangible. Proudly hold up your prop as a
"show-and-tell" item.

Explain a plan

To move someone from simply being informed to feeling comfortable accepting your recommendation, explain an easy-to-follow list of the key elements of the plan, policy, program, approach.

Enter the comfort zone

Encourage a decision-maker to welcome your ideas by including your standards and track record for quality, precision, or safety.

Give direction

Indicate a clear "action plan"—tell the listeners what you want them to do. Help them visualize consequences of acting and not acting.

Get on the same page

Build trust and mutual understanding by starting with areas of agreement before tackling unfamiliar or controversial areas.

Establish common ground

Relate your proposal, plan, or concept to the values held by the general listeners as well as by the decision-makers. Put your own perspectives aside and build on where you have common ideals and principles.

Move decision-makers to action

Since there is no universal technique to influence decision-makers, make your presentation an *unforgettable* experience.

Assemble the pieces that cultivate an atmosphere for decision-making:

TIP #69

- Position your message firmly in the decision-maker's mind with a memorable theme or slogan.

- Propose the specific line of action to take.

- Present yourself as an "approachable authority."

- Choose colors and styles for clothing and graphics that set the "right" tone.

- Arrange seating to accommodate political sensitivities and power personalities.

Name it!

When you regularly use a process or procedure that reliably produces results (such as monitoring budgets, measuring progress, securing safety), give it a name. Label it as your unique system for accomplishing the task.

Conquer Q&A: 5 Ways

"How-To" for Client Meetings

Presenting to Win!

Find a perfect place

When possible, select the presentation environment you prefer so you can be at your personal best. If you don't want people to be distracted while you talk, try not to be scheduled around a meal. If you work best by creating a close audience rapport, request a conference room setting and avoid using a podium.

Stress the significance

As you discuss each main point, insert a statement reinforcing its importance. You can be so blunt as to say: "This is important because … " or "The advantage of this approach is … "

Hold 'em

To hold the audience's active attention and interest throughout a presentation, break your overall timeslot into modules of varying lengths. Explore how each module could feature a different presenter, form of media, pacing, or technique for engagement.

TIP #74

Create memory

Establish a theme that encapsulates your message:

- Use 2–8 words.

- Make it memorable.

- Make it upbeat.

- Repeat it throughout.

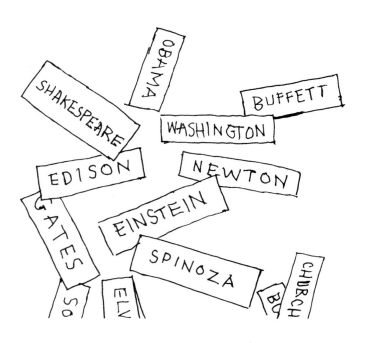

114

Name drop!

Help your remarks take on importance in a larger, broader context. Refer to resources that support your points by quoting people, places, articles, publications, research, authorities, celebrities, literature, news sources, lawmakers, renowned colleagues, university professors, trusted local people, and so on.

TIP #76

Structural approach: 1

To build the argument for your proposed line of action, suggest the preferred approach/decision up front and then spend the rest of the presentation proving why it is preferred.

Structural approach: 2

To build the argument for your proposed line of action, present a series of statements that encourage the listener to agree. With each "yes" nod of the head, the momentum builds, leading to your conclusion, "If you want this result, then let's proceed as I suggest."

TIP #78

Jargon? Maybe

Use professional terminology thoughtfully:

- Be aware of which words and phrases are specific to your field and would be unfamiliar to others.

- You may use jargon cautiously with lay people, particularly when you need to assert your expertise or when no other words can explain as effectively. If you do use a term, define it immediately.

Paint a picture

Get results by explaining your message with language that paints a picture in the mind of the listener. Help listeners picture how things will be once a decision is made, policy is adopted, or the next step is taken. Be specific, descriptive, not flowery. And, don't overdo it! Just one well-crafted sentence can cement the whole thought.

TIP #80

Jargon? The glue

Use your terminology confidently when the audience is in your same line of work, involved in the same cause, has similar training, or has plenty of experience in working with people in your field. Jargon promotes instant bonding and connection, smoothing the way for decision-making.

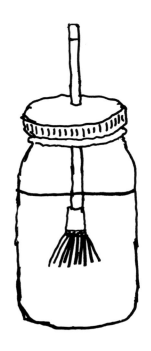

Qualify and quantify

Tighten loose language that can cause misinterpretation and unrealistic expectations. Definitions of "relative" terms, such as beautiful, large, nearby, crowded, state-of-the-art, change with a person's own experience. To assure you and your audience share the same understandings, qualify and quantify when you use such terms. Give specifics: how large is large?; crowded compared to what?; state-of-the-art in what context?

Guide with words

Sprinkle your remarks with language that "guides" thinking. Find words that transfer your passion, that motivate and excite others. Try borrowing language from advertisements. Used sparingly, guiding words give the perfect boost to regular, straightforward explanations or otherwise flat discussions.

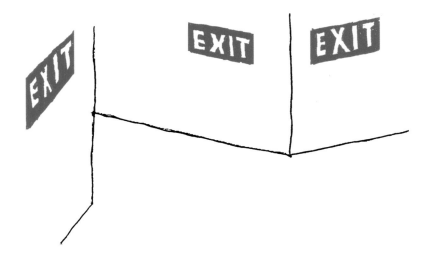

TIP #83

Tame reluctance

Compare. Comparison helps the reluctant or skeptical feel more confident. Compare the unfamiliar (that which you are suggesting) to the familiar—something the listeners have experienced or can become familiar with actually or virtually.

Intrigue with transitions

Intrigue as you introduce each new section of your presentation. Ask a question as you begin the next topic. Open with a quote from someone you admire. Change media. Relay an anecdote. Re-spark audience interest as you begin each new aspect of your talk.

Watch your step!

Keep aware that as much as 65 percent of the message comes across not in the brilliance of what you say, but rather in the non-verbal messages.

No jokes, please

Do not open with a joke. Jokes used to "warm up the audience" are superfluous, can dilute the impact of your message, and distract from your mission.

No-dry zone

Inject *natural* humor—occasionally. As you do, smile but never laugh at your own one-liners or clever-isms. Just roll on with your remarks, taking the humorous remark in stride. Let the listeners do the laughing.

Include the rich and famous

Use endorsements and testimonials to add an element of credibility or glamour. Acquire these specifically solicited statements of endorsement as they work magic in garnering support for your cause.

TIP #89

Tune in and edit

Pay attention both to your performance *and* *simultaneously* to how each person is reacting. *Read* the reactions. Be prepared to be flexible so you can edit the content or adjust your delivery on the spot.

Maximize time

Be direct. Be organized. Be memorable.

Make your point clear. Make your point *clearly*.

Give examples and relay anecdotes succinctly.

Smile.

Project stature

To project stature, stand and sit "tall."
No leaning. No intensely holding the podium.
Let your hands be free for gesturing. Let your
stance show confidence and competence.

Wing it?

Practice your presentation!

Remember, if you are good at "winging it," your presentation will sound like a good "winged" presentation. Is that what you want? You *can* build practice time into your schedule:

- Practice small portions of the whole.

- Practice silently to yourself at random times.

- Practice one segment at a time.

Make it inviting

Present complex ideas in simple ways.
Make intricate information easy to acquire.

- Use inviting renderings and uncomplicated graphics.

- Select vocabulary that encourages understanding.

- Choose visuals, props, body language, and voice that work together to make information comfortable to grasp and remember.

TIP #94

Deliver the subject matter!

- Add marketing-style words and phrases to create interest.

- Put your hand motions, body movements, and facial expressions to work to illustrate your points.

- Dress for the image you want to project.

- Use vocal intonations to make important recommendations sound reasoned, conversational, and sincere.

If it moves, stop talking

When including computer animation, video clips, Internet feeds, and so on, let the visuals speak for themselves. Resist the temptation to talk over them to explain what's going on.

Steps:

1   Give an overview of what you are about to show.

2   Explain the specific items viewers should be looking for.

3   Play the animation and do not talk—let viewers watch.

4   Pause the action to make a comment or refocus attention on a different aspect.

5   Give a verbal review of the main ideas at the end of the animation.

Be handy

Don't point. Use a strong, open hand to serve as an exclamation point to punctuate a key statement.

Show you know

Anticipate questions *before* they are asked and include the answers in the body of your presentation.

Inspire curiosity

Grab and hold attention by keeping listeners curious. Group information into unusual categories and label each category with a thought-provoking, creative, or unexpected title.

Plan before you speak

Eight planning steps:

- **State**: intended outcome.

- **Investigate**: arrangement of the meeting space.

- **Analyze**: the listener profiles and motives.

- **Articulate**: the topic, task, or situation as a problem to be solved.

- **Identify**: listener benefits.

- **List**: main points to make.

- **Determine**: the "image" you want to project.

- **Select**: an array of presentation approaches, media/technology.

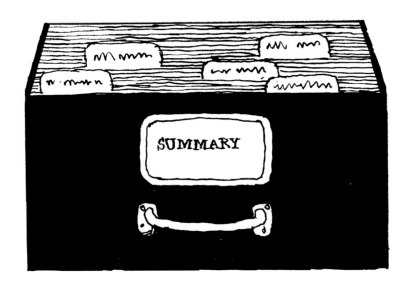

TIP #100

"Thank you" is not an ending

Presenters tend to think that "thank you" is the way to conclude. Thank you is polite. Thank you is nice. Thank you has no impact. Instead, end with a single, dynamic, high-energy sentence that encapsulates your theme and states the action you want taken. After that, if you want to say thank you, do so as a separate gesture of appreciation.

Thank You

Ask Joanne

Frequently asked
questions from one-on-one
coaching sessions

Q: *Should I use a laser pointer?*

A: Yes and no.

Yes, use a laser pointer if you are at great distance from your visual and can hold the pointer VERY still. Point slowly and leave the red dot on the specific detail for a full three seconds or longer.

No, do not use a laser pointer if you are in a smaller-sized conference room or if you want to create a personalized rapport with the listeners.

Q: *I don't get many opportunities to give formal presentations. How will I ever improve if my presentations are so infrequent?*

A: Consider every meeting with two or more people an opportunity to present. Try out the various techniques I have shared with you by putting them into action at a regular meeting, or when just giving a project update, a quick progress report, or sharing research results. Any time you are delivering information is a time to practice your presentation skills.

Q: *I usually rush at the end to fit my whole presentation into the time limit. How can I fix this?*

A: Practice. Practice with a stopwatch or alarm clock. Do a timed practice several times. With each practice, cut and edit so you learn how much information fits into specific time blocks. A shorter presentation that fits comfortably in the assigned time slot has great impact. Too much information crammed into any time slot becomes too rushed and gets tuned out.

Q: *I get so nervous that I forget what I'm going to say. My mind just goes blank. Is there anything I can do?*

A: Your presentation visuals, the ones you show to the audience, can also serve as your own notecards. The bullet points should be just enough of a prompt to remind you what to say.

Bring in items to demonstrate the points you will be making. When you lift up the item to show to the audience, you can focus on explaining the item, its importance, and its relevance to the topic, until you get yourself back on track.

Q: *My mouth gets dry as I am presenting. What do you think about the speaker drinking water during a presentation?*

A: Many presenters need to drink water, as you probably have noticed. Just be sure the water is room temperature or lukewarm (not the ice water that is usually provided), because the lukewarm water gently moistens the palate and soothes the vocal chords.

Q: *I get such stagefright that I start shaking and feel like I will collapse. What suggestions do you have?*

A: There are a couple of physical techniques you can try. Steady your shaking hands by intentionally using them to illustrate a point you are making—show the size or shape of something. Point to some specific detail or word on your visuals. Do so with your muscles tensed and arms extended so you are really using your nervous energy.

Be conscious to tighten your leg muscles so you keep your presentation posture and stand firm.

Q: *I do practice my presentations until they are perfect, but something is missing to make me feel confident. What else can I do?*

A: After you have rehearsed to your satisfaction, take a non-stressed few moments to close your eyes and visualize yourself in the presentation setting. Picture yourself as accurately as you can, from the moment you enter the room, all the way through the presentation to the conclusion and the applause.

Q: *The audience will not be able to fully appreciate my slide presentations unless the lights are off, but then I can't see my own notes. This is a problem! What do you suggest?*

A: Always present with the lights on—even if you have them on low. When you darken the room, you encourage the audience to be too relaxed! Check your slides in advance to make sure they look the way you want them to in a room with some light. The more light in the room, the better.

Q: *I don't usually wear a suit to work. Should I wear one for the presentation?*

A: Rule one: dress for the image your company wants to project.

Q: *I usually read my prepared presentation so I don't make any mistakes or forget what I am going to say. Is that OK?*

A: Yes and no.

No, it is not okay to read a prepared presentation word-for-word because it keeps you from creating audience rapport and usually results in boring, dry delivery.

Yes, it is okay to read if you focus on vocal expression, add vitality, and know the content so well that you can maintain real eye contact with the audience about 75 percent of the time.

Q: *What is the one bit of advice I should always remember?*

A: Never go in unprepared.

FAQs

Q: *I need to use notes. Is that OK?*

A: Of course it is okay to use notes. It is how you use them that is important. Experiment with different formats for your notes: flipchart, presentation boards, slides, 8 ½ x 11 sheets on a clipboard, whatever. Practice with your notes so your delivery is smooth and lively. Your notes should not be a crutch, but rather a quick reminder of what you plan to say.

Make your notes a natural, comfortable part of your delivery.

Q: *Should I take questions during my presentation? What do you recommend?*

A: The danger with allowing questions throughout your presentation is that the question can take you off track and gobble valuable time allotted for the points you planned to make. If you are good at giving brief responses and getting yourself back on topic, then take a few questions. Since, however, it is an interruption to your flow and content, I actually do not recommend it. But also, you must assess whether it is important for you, for political reasons, to allow interruptions.

Q: *I want to really impress my committee right at the outset. What one hint do you have for how I should begin my presentation?*

A: Do not begin with, "Today I am going to talk about …"

Q: *Although I speak English fluently, Japanese is my first language. What would you suggest I do to make sure everyone will understand me?*

A: Work very hard to speak slowly and clearly. Say fewer things than you might want to say. Give shorter explanations. Speak in shorter sentences and also stretch out each sentence so it is slower in delivery. Take your time so you can enunciate precisely.

Q: *I want to pass around handout materials during my presentation. What is the best way to do this?*

A: The best time to distribute handout materials is before you begin or after you have concluded. Passing around materials while you are speaking becomes a distraction and steals the attention from you.

About the illustrator

Bob Gill is an illustrator, designer, filmmaker, writer, and teacher. He was the Gill in Fletcher/Forbes/Gill, which later became Pentagram, one of the most important design partnerships in the world.

About the author

Joanne G. Linowes, founder of Boston-based Linowes Executive Development Institute (LXDi), is the originator of internationally renowned techniques for impressive and winning presentations, as well as communications skills for business development and client relations. She conducts high-caliber, results-focused professional development programs, leadership training, and executive coaching. Her expertise, since 1986, is in working with executives and managers in design, engineering, construction, sciences, technical and quantitative fields, healthcare, legal, and financial services.

Ms. Linowes is a popular, dynamic speaker at professional conferences and regularly publishes articles in trade publications. Earlier, she was an award-winning television producer and promotion director for programs on WGBH-TV, the PBS television network, and NPR National Public Radio.

Ms. Linowes has a B.S. from Boston University and a M.S. from The University of Pennsylvania. She is also the author of *Acquiring the Competitive Edge: Essential Communications Strategies for Design Professionals*.

Index of topics